BACKPACKER.

Using A
GPS

D0711616

Digital Trip Planning, Recording, and Sharing

Bruce Grubbs

FALCONGUIDES

GUILFORD, CONNECTICUT
HELENA, MONTANA

AN IMPRINT OF GLOBE PEQUOT PRESS

FALCONGUIDES®

Copyright © 2011 by Morris Book Publishing, LLC

Backpacker is a registered trademark of Cruz Bay Publishing, Inc.
FalconGuides is an imprint of Globe Pequot Press.
Falcon, FalconGuides, and Outfit Your Mind are registered trademarks of Morris
Book Publishing, LLC.
TOPO! Explorer maps courtesy of National Geographic Maps (www.natgeomaps
.com)
DeLorme maps courtesy of DeLorme Topo North America (www.delorme.com)
Magellan maps courtesy of Magellan (www.magellan.com)
Google maps courtesy of Google Earth (www.earth.google.com)
Photos by Bruce Grubbs unless otherwise noted.

Project editor: David Legere
Text design: Sheryl P. Kober
Layout: Kevin Mak

Library of Congress Cataloging-in-Publication Data is available on file.

ISBN 978-0-7627-5655-1

Printed in China

10 9 8 7 6 5 4 3 2 1

Contents

Introduction

Why use a computer and a Global Positioning System (GPS) receiver to plan, record, and share your outdoor experiences? Well, because it's fun. It's also useful. Digital maps give you the ability to accurately measure distance and elevation change so you can plan a trip to suit you exactly. The ability to record your route precisely on the trip and then view it at home on the computer in three dimensions on topographic maps and satellite photos adds a new perspective to your outdoor adventure. Then you can share your trip, your comments, and your photos and videos with other outdoor enthusiasts via the Web, an activity known as "e-hiking."

This book focuses on navigation for self-propelled outdoor activities such as hiking, backpacking, paddling, sea kayaking, road cycling, mountain biking, fishing, camping, and anything else you do in the outdoors using muscle power. While much of this information may be useful to other users, I don't address such specialized GPS applications as marine or aviation use.

In this book the term "maps" means digital maps (maps generated on a computer screen) unless I say otherwise. I also refer to maps for recreational activities, such as government or commercial topographic (topo) or recreation maps. Although the screen shots and photos are necessarily of one particular digital map program and GPS brand and model, I'm not endorsing anyone's product. Instead, I point out the features that are useful and how to put them to practical use. (All product and model names are the trademarks of their manufacturers.)

If you plan to use your GPS receiver primarily with paper maps instead of digital maps, take a look at my other GPS book, *Basic Essentials Using GPS*. It

Using a GPS unit can help guide you on your hikes. Hold the unit flat and above your waist so you don't lose the signal.

discusses paper map, handheld compass, and GPS work in a practical and easy to understand format with plenty of real-world examples.

GPS techniques complement traditional outdoor navigation techniques using map and compass, and are not a substitute for those skills. Remember, never rely solely on electronic navigation in the outdoors. If you need a refresher, check out *Backpacker* magazine's *Trailside Navigation* and *Basic Illustrated Map and Compass,* both FalconGuides published by Globe Pequot Press.

Chapter One
Digital Maps

Digital maps are the basis for planning, recording, saving, and sharing your outdoor trips. Such maps can either be off-line—map data on CD, DVD, or your hard drive—or online-accessible through the Internet. Off-line maps can be used anywhere, even when you don't have Internet access, and the maps can be updated when you are back online. Online maps are maintained by the provider and require high-speed Internet access.

Maps can be planimetric, showing primarily man-made features such as roads, or topographic (topo), showing the terrain and natural features as well as man-made features. Planimetric maps are mainly useful with street GPS. Topo maps are much better for planning and recording backcountry travel with trail GPS.

Digital maps can be produced by scanning map images or by drawing vector graphics from digital map and elevation data. U.S. Geological Survey (USGS) topo maps, which are the most detailed and accurate maps, are available as more than 20,000 scanned bitmap images covering the entire United States. Unfortunately, because there are so many maps to maintain, they have not been frequently updated. Natural features such as rivers, mountains, and canyons rarely change and are shown accurately, but man-made features such as roads, trails, and structures may be out of date.

Vector maps are generated in the computer from digital map data, which comes from both government and private sources. Vector maps don't show topography as well as USGS topo maps, but man-made features are updated more often, and that makes vector maps useful for city and road navigation, as well as finding trailheads and following well-defined trails. In practice, scanned and vector maps complement each other, and the outdoor digital map user should have both.

PRINTED MAPS

U.S. Geological Survey (USGS)

USGS, the federal agency charged with producing and maintaining topographic maps of the entire country, sells standard paper topographic maps at http://store.usgs.gov at current government prices. You can also download topos for free in PDF format. You can print each map on four sheets of letter-size paper, or as a single sheet with a wide-format printer or plotter.

MyTopo.com

At www.MyTopo.com, you can print custom, waterproof, but expensive topo maps for anywhere in the United States and Canada.

DIGITAL MAP AND GPS TOOLS

These include programs that ship with map DVDs or CDs, as well as software that lets you download maps to your hard drive for use off-line. Most of the programs that supply maps on optical media let you update the maps online. Other programs are Web-based, so you need a high-speed Internet connection to use the maps. Prices, especially for the maps themselves, vary from free to expensive and change rapidly, so shop around. These programs work with most GPS units, but check to make certain your unit is supported before buying. Also check that map coverage is available for your area of interest.

DeLorme Topo North America

Topo North America (www.delorme.com) is available on DVD for most of North America, and in subsets. It displays vector topo maps in a wide range of scales. Since you can get the entire country for about twice the price as a single state from National Geographic Topo!, Topo North America is a good map set for areas where you don't need detailed scanned topo maps, and for road, street, and trail coverage. At extra cost you can download portions of scanned USGS 1:24,000 topos, which DeLorme calls "3DTopoQuads," as well as satellite imagery. A variety of tools lets you draw routes, mark waypoints, create routes, draw shapes, measure distance and area, and add notes to your maps. Topo North America is designed for use with DeLorme Earthmate GPS units, and it works with most other GPS units.

This vector map from DeLorme Topo North America obviously has less detail than a scanned map but does show the Escalante Route, a relatively new trail southwest of Tanner Canyon Rapids that is not shown on the USGS topo.
© 2010 DeLorme (www.delorme.com) Topo North America 9.0 ®

EasyGPS

EasyGPS (www.easygps.com) is a free GPS mapping program from TopoGrafix that lets you transfer waypoints, routes, and tracks between your computer and GPS. It maps the GPS data on-screen but does not use topo maps. It's a good tool for archiving your GPS data in the standard GPX format.

ExpertGPS

Also from TopoGrafix, ExpertGPS (www.expertgps .com) uses online USGS topo maps and aerial imagery as base maps. You can import and export GPS data in GPX format, and a variety of tools lets you draw routes and add map symbols and text notes to the maps. ExpertGPS can import and export GPS data in a wide variety of formats. You can try the program free for thirty days.

Fugawi

Fugawi (www.fugawi.com) makes GPS and topo mapping software for use with their topo maps. Coverage includes much of the world. Maps are downloaded to your hard drive for use off-line.

Garmin Topo US 100K and 24K

Like DeLorme's Topo North America, Garmin Topo US 100K (www.garmin.com) covers the entire country but without as much detail. Garmin Topo US 24K offers regional 1:24,000 vector topo maps. Garmin's maps are designed primarily for use with their mapping GPS receivers.

Magellan

Magellan (www.magellangps.com) produces topo maps for use with their GPS receivers. Their topo coverage includes Canada and Mexico as well as the United States, and they are starting to produce topos of Europe as well.

Maptech

Maptech (www.maptech.com) makes Terrain Navigator software and produces topo maps for the United States on CD and DVD. They also have free online browsable maps.

National Geographic Topo!

Topo! (www.natgeomaps.com) uses 1:500,000, 1:100,000, and 1:24,000 high-resolution scanned USGS topos that can be seamlessly displayed and printed. Topo! is available in sets of CDs that cover entire western states and regional sets of smaller states. Two smaller-scale National Geographic planimetric map levels are used as locator maps and are also useful as road maps. A variety of tools lets you draw routes, mark waypoints, create routes, and add notes and photos to your maps. Topo! works with most GPS units.

U.S. Geological Survey

At the USGS online store (http://store.usgs.gov), you can download free topo maps in PDF format. These

can be used with programs, such as Fugawi (www
.fugawi.com), that allow import of scanned maps or
maps in PDF format.

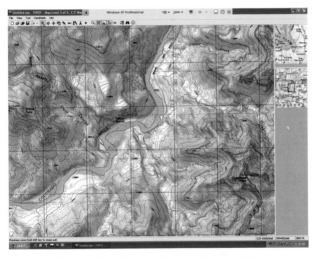

This map displayed in National Geographic Topo! is based on a
high-resolution scan of a 1:24000-scale USGS topographic map;
which are the most detailed maps available for the U.S. Optional
shaded relief is turned on, which highlights and shades the terrain as if the sun was shining from the upper right. Shaded relief is
especially helpful when you are first learning to read topo maps.
TOPO! © NATIONAL GEOGRAPHIC

TRIP-SHARING WEB SITES

These sites allow you to upload your GPS trip data,
including photos and video, and share it with others.
You can also download trip data for your own use.
These sites are evolving rapidly, and more sites are

appearing all the time. If your GPS trip data is for anything beyond casual use, back it up on your own computer using GPX format and software such as EasyGPS or National Geographic Topo! Since most of these trips are uploaded by users, the quality varies, and you should cross-check the information with printed maps, guidebooks, and best of all, a friend or ranger who's been there. The best sites allow users to rate or review the trips.

Backpacker Magazine

Backpacker magazine's destinations Web page (www.backpacker.com/destinations), in conjunction with Trimble Outdoors, features trips uploaded and rated by the magazine staff, readers, and other sources. You can share trips by e-mail, texting to cell phones, embedding the trip map on your Web site, or by sharing bookmarks on any of the popular bookmark-sharing sites. You can download trips to your iPhone, Android phone, Web account, GPS phone, your computer in GPX format, and Google Earth in KML format. Tools allow you to plan a trip online and upload a GPX file to a Garmin GPS receiver. (Disclaimer: This book is published by *Backpacker* magazine and Globe Pequot Press.)

EveryTrail

EveryTrail (www.everytrail.com) features road trips as well as backcountry trips, uploaded and rated by users. You can share EveryTrail trips on your Web site, by e-mail and instant messaging, and via GPX and Google Earth KML files.

Google Earth

Google Earth (http://earth.google.com) has the most detailed satellite photography available in a free application, and it is regularly updated. Tools allow you to annotate images, attach videos, mark locations, create and import GPS data in GPX and KML formats, and tag photos. This process is not as seamless as it could be, often requiring multiple steps or intermediate Web sites.

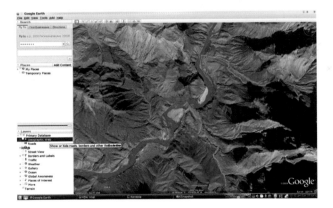

Google Earth features satellite imagery of the entire planet that can be zoomed, panned, and tilted for a 3D view.

MapMyFitness.com

This site is aimed primarily at tracking physical fitness activities such as running and cycling. Apps are available for the iPhone and Blackberry smartphones.

National Geographic Topo! Explorer

Topo! Explorer offers the functionality of National Geographic Topo! State Series maps in an online format. You can use Topo! Explorer via a Web browser, but to use all of the program's features you'll need to download the PC or Mac software from www.topo.com. You can download "superquads,"

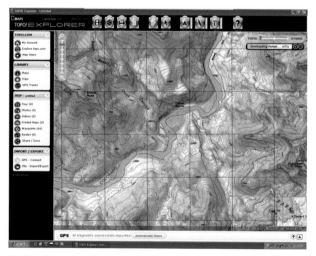

National Geographic Topo! Explorer uses scanned USGS "super-quads," which can be viewed as a normal topo map, aerial imagery, or a hybrid of the two.

TOPO! EXPLORER © 2010 NATIONAL GEOGRAPHIC

which are a combination of USGS 1:24,000 topo maps and aerial photography, and also use any Topo! State Series maps you have. Unfortunately, covering the area for an ambitious trip quickly gets very expensive.

Trimble Outdoors

Trimble (www.trimbleoutdoors.com) is similar to *Backpacker* magazine's site but focuses on trips uploaded and rated by users.

Chapter Two
Buying a GPS

Though GPS receivers continue to evolve as the technology is constantly improved, there are basic features to look for and compare when buying a GPS for recording your outdoor adventures. Manufacturer Web sites are the best places to compare specifications.

Comparing Magellan GPS units using the comparison feature at www.magellangps.com. This is the easiest way to pick out the features that you want.

© 2010 MAGELLAN

STREET OR TRAIL GPS OR CELL PHONE

Street GPS receivers are touch screen mapping units optimized for road navigation. They come with street and point of interest (POI) databases covering defined regions such as the United States, Europe, or Australia. The unit typically displays a planimetric map of your current location and the names of the streets around you, and gives turn-by-turn driving directions visually on the screen and verbally. Since streets and POIs change frequently, you should get a unit that allows the database to be updated. Although many street GPS units have a walking mode, they usually feature planimetric maps and use internal, proprietary rechargeable batteries. Though very useful for urban navigation on foot, they are not practical for backcountry trips.

A trail GPS is a handheld unit primarily intended for portable use in the outdoors. Most units have a battery life of twenty hours or more of continuous use; that can be stretched to many days if the GPS is turned on only to record waypoints and check your position. Plus, most trail GPS units use standard AA or AAA batteries, so you can carry spares. Many trail GPS units let you load street maps and POI databases for use on the road, but their screens are smaller than street GPS displays, and most don't give voice prompts.

GPS-enabled smartphones can be used as GPS road or trail navigators by downloading apps. Some apps are free and others must be purchased. Apps for iPhone include Google Maps, MobileNavigator, Garmin Mobile 20, TomTom for iPhone, Magellan Roadmate, iTopoMaps, Gaia GPS, and TopoPoint USA. For Android-based phones there is Google Maps, CoPilot Live, Velox Pro, NavDroyd, Gaia GPS, and Topo Maps. Blackberry apps include Google Maps, Topo! Explorer, NavFunPro, LifeInPocket, and WisePilot Navigation. Palm apps include Google Maps, NavPro, Flare, and Locate-A-Rama. Some Nokia phones include free road navigation with Ovi Maps; apps include Google Maps and others. Windows Mobile apps include Google Maps and CoPilot Live.

There are many other GPS apps—check the app stores for the latest:

- » www.apple.com/iphone/apps-for-iphone
- » www.android.com/market
- » http://na.blackberry.com/eng/services/appworld
- » www.palm.com/us/products/software/mobile-applications.html
- » www.nokiausa.com/ovi-services-and-apps
- » www.microsoft.com/windowsmobile/en-us/downloads/default.mspx

Backpacker magazine's Web site also has smartphone apps (www.backpacker.com). Also check www.google.com/mobile/maps.

The advantage of this approach is that you can download maps and GPS trip data directly to your phone for use on the trail. You can also upload trip data directly to trip-sharing Web sites from your phone, when in cell phone data range. The downsides are that you can quickly run out of battery power, and the GPS receiver is designed for locating the phone during a 911 call, not for navigation. Consider carrying spare batteries, an external battery pack, or a solar charger to charge your phone's proprietary batteries. Most phones let you turn off the phone function (often called airplane mode), which will save battery power. Dedicated trail GPS receivers have more sensitive GPS receivers and are reliable. If you will be depending on your GPS receiver in a remote area, buy a trail GPS.

MAPPING CAPABILITY

Mapping GPS units come with base maps of defined regions. Look for a mapping, trail-type GPS that will accept uploaded topo and street maps as well as POI databases, and that uses Secure Digital High Capacity (SDHC) or mini Secure Digital (mini-SD) memory cards for storing maps and GPS data.

HIGH-SENSITIVITY RECEIVER

Most current GPS units have high-sensitivity, multi-channel parallel receivers that receive as many as thirty-two channels simultaneously. These units are noticeably better than older receivers at maintaining their satellite lock under difficult conditions such as heavy forest cover. This is especially important for e-hiking, where you leave the GPS on continuously to record an unbroken track.

WAAS

The Wide Area Augmentation System is used to improve the accuracy of GPS from the civilian standard of 33 feet (10 meters), which is limited by atmospheric effects. It works by receiving signals from differential GPS transmitters that are placed on precisely surveyed points. These transmitters measure the difference between their known locations and the GPS-derived location and transmit the error correction to the GPS unit.

Most receivers have WAAS capability built in, using satellite signals provided by the Federal Aviation Administration (FAA) for aircraft navigation, resulting in accuracy of 10 feet (3 meters) or better. FAA WAAS can only be used when the GPS unit has an unobstructed view of the sky down to the horizon. Other WAAS systems are set up locally by the U.S. Coast Guard for ship navigation in coastal waters, and by government and private organizations to provide accuracy down to millimeters for surveying and other specialized uses.

WAAS accuracy is not needed for road or outdoor navigation. Because using WAAS uses more power, it should be turned off when the unit is running on batteries.

BATTERY TYPE AND LIFE

Street GPS units use internal rechargeable batteries that are not user-replaceable because they are intended to run on vehicle power. Most trail GPS receivers use two standard AA or AAA alkaline, lithium, or rechargeable nickel-metal hydride (NiMH) batteries. Some smartphones use proprietary rechargeable batteries that can be replaced by the user, but others, such as the iPhone, have internal batteries that are not user-replaceable. Since continuous use for GPS and mapping depletes the batteries in a couple of hours, at present smartphones are not practical for all-day or multiday treks.

NiMH batteries are more environmentally responsible and far cheaper in the long run than single-use alkaline or lithium cells—they are the best choice for day trips and whenever you have access to a charger. Solar chargers are available for backcountry use. Lithium single-use cells are the lightest and longest-lasting solution for extended backcountry trips when there is no way to recharge batteries.

WATERPROOFNESS

The majority of GPS receivers are waterproof, but you shouldn't depend on the waterproofing in harsh environments such as sea kayaking. Get a waterproof deck bag with a transparent window that lets you operate the unit without removing it. Land travelers can use a zippered storage bag.

Being waterproof doesn't guarantee the unit will float. Some do, some don't. A waterproof bag is also good insurance to make sure your expensive GPS doesn't disappear into the depths.

COMPUTER INTERFACE

Look for a USB 2.0 or better interface, which is essential for transferring data between the computer and the GPS, as well as updating the receiver's software and maps. Serial and USB 1.1 interfaces are obsolete.

AUTOMATIC ROAD ROUTING

All street GPS units and most mapping-type trail GPSs have automatic turn-by-turn road routing, allowing you to follow roads to a selected destination. Generally, to have road routing on a trail GPS, you'll have to install optional street mapping.

ELECTRONIC COMPASS

All trail GPS units show your heading (direction of travel) on a compass page while you're moving. At walking speeds the heading information can be erratic because the GPS calculates your heading from a series of position fixes. These fixes can be a second apart, which causes the computed heading to vary. At higher speeds, such as mountain biking or driving, the heading is accurate. The solution for trail use is an electronic compass, which takes over from the GPS at low speeds. Some electronic compasses have to be held horizontal when in use, like their mechanical counterparts, but the latest GPS receivers have three-axis compasses that can be used while tilted.

BAROMETRIC ALTIMETER

Although all GPS receivers compute altitude, it's only accurate to +/-100 feet (30 meters). A GPS with a built-in barometric altimeter is accurate to +/-10 feet (3 meters) and can be used to record an elevation profile of your trip and also to watch for weather changes.

GEOCACHING MODE

This mode uses special icons to display geocaches on the GPS map page and allows you to mark a geocache as found and to enter notes. Most units can also directly download geocache data from the Web. See the "Geocaching" chapter for details.

SUN AND MOON INFORMATION

Many GPS receivers give information on sunrise, sunset, and moon phases. This information is useful to many outdoorspeople, especially hunters, anglers, photographers, and sea kayakers.

TIDE TABLES

Sea kayakers in particular need tide information for planning trips around the tidal currents and avoiding hazardous tidal rip areas. Seacoast hikers need tide information because some coastal hikes are impassible at high tide, and to avoid becoming trapped below cliffs by an incoming tide. Anglers and other marine users will also want this feature. Most units show a graph of tide stages for any selected point.

CUSTOM POINTS OF INTEREST

All street GPS units and most mapping trail units allow you download additional points of interest (POI) for new areas. POIs change frequently, so the database should be updated for any major road trip. You can also save and name your favorite locations as searchable POIs.

UNIT TO UNIT TRANSFER

Wireless transfer allows you to send GPS data directly to another wireless GPS without having to transfer the data through a computer. This is an easy way to make sure all the GPS receivers in your party have the same route data before a trip. All units must be compatible models from the same manufacturer.

Smartphone GPS apps have the ability to e-mail mapping data, so you can send information from the field to your home computer—if you have a cell phone data signal.

OTHER NAVIGATION EQUIPMENT

Maps

Don't depend solely on maps loaded into your GPS, no matter how detailed. If your batteries die or the unit fails, you'll need printed maps to find your way. Printed recreation and trail maps also often have information not available on GPS maps.

Compass

For the same reasons, always carry a good quality, handheld, liquid-filled compass with a mapping baseplate as a backup. A compass with a declination offset is easier to use because it compensates for magnetic variation and reads in true bearings that can be used directly on a map.

Chapter Three

Setting Up Your GPS

STREET GPS

Vehicle Mounting

You will need to mount the receiver where its built-in antenna has a clear view of the sky and where both the driver and the front seat passenger can see the screen. Most street GPS units come with a mounting bracket that uses a suction cup to mount the unit to

This street GPS is mounted on the dashboard with a suction cup mount on an adhesive disk. Note how it doesn't obscure the windshield.

the windshield. In some states, mounting anything on the windshield is against the law, and you'll need to mount the receiver on the dashboard. There is a wide variety of aftermarket mounting systems.

A power cord, which should be supplied with the unit, plugs into a cigarette lighter power socket. Save the batteries for use away from the vehicle.

Initializing

Street GPS setup is simple. Take the unit outdoors where it has a clear view of the sky and turn it on. Wait for the satellite status screen to show that the

This street GPS startup screen shows the satellite status in the upper left corner. Green bars mean the unit has locked onto enough satellites to navigate, while red bars mean the unit cannot navigate and you need to move to a location with a better view of the sky. The battery charge indicator is in the upper right, with four green bars indicating that the internal battery is fully charged.

GPS is ready to navigate. This process takes a minute or two if the unit is new or hasn't been used in a while.

TRAIL GPS

Setting up a trail GPS takes a little longer than a street GPS. There are a number of options you'll want to set up to customize the receiver for your use. Many of these options also apply to smartphone GPS apps.

Installing Batteries

Use rechargeable NiMH batteries if your GPS accepts them. For situations where weight is critical, such as backpacking, use single-use lithium batteries. They are lighter than NiMH or alkaline batteries and work better in cold weather.

Battery life can be extended by setting the unit to battery saver mode, if it has one. At night, use the lowest backlight settings. Always carry a backup set of batteries.

The battery saver mode is selected on the main setup page on this GPS and should be used when running on battery power. This GPS unit also lets you select the battery type, so you won't get false low-battery indications when using rechargeable NiMH batteries. These batteries operate at a lower voltage than single-use batteries.

Initializing

Take the unit outdoors where it has a clear view of the sky and switch it on. After a startup page the satellite status page will appear, and the receiver will start searching the sky for satellites. This process normally takes a little longer the first time, or if the GPS hasn't been used in a while. Wait until the unit has a 3D fix before turning it off.

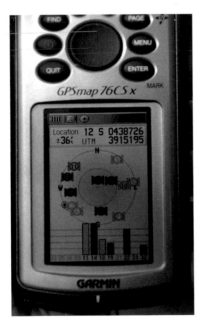

During initial setup, wait until the GPS receiver has locked on to at least four satellites and has a 3D position. This unit is locked on to six satellites.

Time Format and Zone

Although all GPS units pick up the correct time from the GPS satellites, you may want to change the time display settings. GPS uses Universal Time Coordinated (UTC), but you can set your local time zone and display the time in either twelve- or twenty-four-hour format.

This GPS allows you to display time in your local time zone by selecting a city or a time zone.

Position Format

GPS uses Universal Transverse Mercator (UTM) coordinates internally, but receivers can display many different coordinate systems. UTM is the best system to use with digital maps, both off-line and online, because it uses a rectangular grid that is easy to visualize and to plot. UTM is the choice for most professional field workers, including geologists, archaeologists, search and rescue teams, and firefighters. You may need latitude and longitude (lat/long) for printed maps without UTM, and for use with Google Earth and other applications that use lat/long.

Set the displayed coordinate system at the top of the units page, and set the map datum to match the one used by your map. You can also change the units used for distance, speed, elevation, temperature, and pressure to match your region.

Map Datum

The map datum is the system of surveyed ground reference points used to create accurate maps. Digital maps use WGS84, the standard worldwide datum for GPS. Paper USGS topo maps generally use NAD27. There are many local datums in different countries. Failure to use the correct datum with paper maps can result in errors of hundreds of feet or even several miles. Accurate maps have the datum printed in the margin.

> **°37'30"**   ⁶28   670 000 FEET
>
> Mapped, edited, and published by the Geological Survey
>
> Control by USGS and NOS/NOAA
>
> Topography by photogrammetric methods from aerial
> photographs taken 1966. Field checked 1967
> Revised by the Bureau of Indian Affairs 1976. Map edited by USGS 1978
>
> Projection and 10,000-foot grid ticks: Arizona coordinate
> system, east zone (transverse Mercator)
> 1000-meter Universal Transverse Mercator grid ticks,
> zone 12, shown in blue. 1927 North American datum
>
> Fine red dashed lines indicate selected fence lines
>
> Where omitted, land lines have not been established
>
> There may be private inholdings within the boundaries of
> the National or State reservations shown on this map

This printed USGS 1:24,000 topo uses NAD27, the 1927 North American Datum.

North Reference

True north is the direction of the geographic north pole, and all maps that are useful for navigation are printed with true north up. Magnetic north is the direction a compass points, which is approximately

On the GPS heading page, set North Reference to True unless you're working with a handheld compass that doesn't have a declination offset. At the bottom of the screen, set the speed and delay for switching to the electronic compass.

the direction of the magnetic north pole. The difference between true and magnetic north in degrees at any given location is the magnetic variation, or declination.

If you need to navigate using a compass without a declination adjustment, such as a marine card–type compass, set the GPS to use magnetic north. Otherwise, use true north.

Calibrating the Compass

If your GPS has a built-in electronic compass, it should be calibrated at the start of a trip and when the receiver is first used. Go to the compass calibration screen and follow the directions. On Garmin units, for example, the compass is calibrated by holding the unit horizontally and slowly making two complete circles.

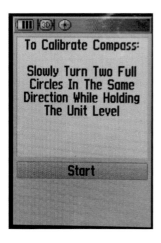

Calibrate the compass at the start of each trip so it will display accurate directions. This unit must be held level when using the electronic compass. The latest GPS receivers don't have this limitation.

Calibrating the Altimeter

GPS units that have a built-in barometric altimeter must be calibrated at the start of a trip and every few hours because air pressure changes constantly with the time of day and passing weather systems. Failure to calibrate the altimeter can result in errors of 500 to 1,000 feet.

To calibrate the altimeter, you must know either your exact elevation or the current sea level–corrected barometric pressure. At home you can get the barometric pressure from your own calibrated barometer or the local National Weather Service (NWS) Web page (www.nws.gov), a weather radio, or by calling the nearest NWS office. In the field, use your elevation as determined from your position on a

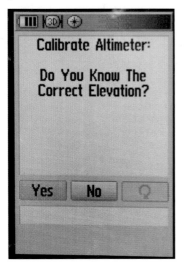

Calibrate the altimeter using your known elevation or the local barometric pressure. Recalibrate every few hours on a trip because barometric pressure changes with the time of day and passing weather systems.

topo map. If you don't know your exact altitude or barometric pressure, you can still use GPS altitude but with less accuracy.

Customizing the Navigation Screens

Most GPS units allow you to customize the information shown on the navigation screens to fit the type of navigating you're doing. A good option is to have the information most useful to you on each page. Avoid duplicate information as much as possible. A possible setup for trail hiking is as follows: On the map screen, display the name and bearing (direction in degrees) of the destination waypoint. On the compass screen, which graphically shows your heading and the bearing to the next waypoint, it's useful to show four data fields—distance and time to the next waypoint, and distance and time to the destination waypoint. On the trip computer page, display total time, moving time, stopped time, maximum speed, moving average speed, current speed, elevation, and odometer.

Chapter Four

Planning Your Trip

DOWNLOADING TRIPS

The easiest way to plan a trip with GPS is to download waypoints, routes, and track data (a series of automatically saved waypoints along your route) from your computer directly to your GPS. You can find GPS trip information on a large number of commercial sites, such as www.trails.com, www.everytrail.com, and www.topo.com, and on free sites such as www.geocaching.com. A good starting point is *Backpacker* magazine's Web site (www.backpacker.com), which has thousands of trips you can download. There are many others and they are changing constantly—do a Web search for GPS trails.

The data downloaded from the Web will usually be in GPX file format on your computer. Geocache data is in LOC format, and digital maps have their own format, such as National Geographic's TPO or DeLorme's TPX.

GPS units commonly come with a program that lets you read GPX and LOC files and send them to your GPS (and download files from the GPS to the computer). There are also free programs such as EasyGPS (www.easygps.com) and GPS Babel (www.gpsbabel.org) that convert between these and many other computer GPS file formats.

Normally you'll download GPS trip data into your digital maps. Since there are so many sources of GPS trip data, some of dubious quality, you should always review and compare the data to other information, such as guidebook descriptions and information from rangers and people who've done the trip. Also look at the number of online reviews of the trip. Never depend on downloaded GPS data alone as your only trip planning and navigation information.

GPS-enabled smartphones with a GPS app can download trip data directly to the phone, bypassing the computer step.

PLOTTING THE ROUTE

You can also plot your own waypoints and routes on digital maps. All the programs come with tools for plotting GPS routes, as well as freehand routes, symbols, and text notes and labels. You can measure distances and directions, too.

Locating a Trailhead on a Street GPS

A street GPS can take you from your starting point to the trailhead, giving verbal and on-screen directions. Since the POI database in street GPS units doesn't usually include trailheads, you'll have to enter it manually. One way is to get the coordinates from another source, such as a guidebook or a recreation map. You may have to convert the coordinates from UTM to lat/long with a digital map program.

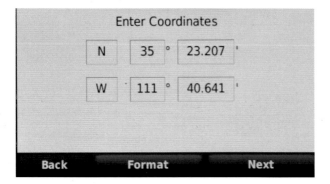

Enter a trailhead in a street GPS by creating a waypoint from lat/long coordinates. The trailhead was located on a recreation map, and the coordinates were taken from a digital topo.

Naming Waypoints and Routes

With digital maps you can start a new route and add waypoints to it by clicking on the map. Put in as many waypoints as you need to follow the twists and turns of the trail, and be sure to put a waypoint at each key point, such as trail junctions, springs, campsites, fishing spots, and any other points of interest.

The program names each waypoint auto-matically starting with a sequence such as 001, 002, 003, etc. It's better to use a descriptive name, within the limitations of your GPS, such as "trailhead." Give your route a descriptive name, too. Doing so makes it easier to use the waypoints and routes on the GPS in the field.

For loop trips, don't use the trailhead or starting waypoint as the ending waypoint, which may confuse your GPS receiver. Instead, place an ending waypoint next to the starting point.

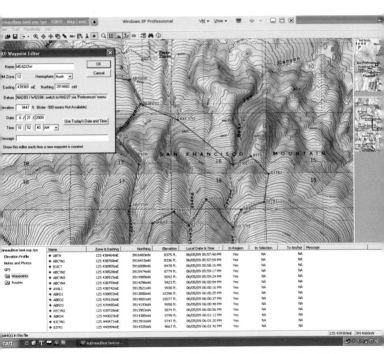

This waypoint has been renamed to Meadow. You can also put a description in the message field. The route, a loop with a cherry stem at the start, is shown in blue, and the small blue diamonds are waypoints. The bottom part of the screen shows the way-points in the order they're encountered on the route.

Plotting the Elevation Profile

Most mapping programs allow you to create an elevation profile (a graph of your route by distance and elevation) by right-clicking the route line. Waypoints are shown along the profile, which lets you see where the long climbs and steep descents are located.

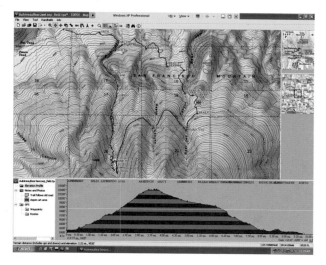

This elevation profile clearly shows the steep, relentless climb at the start of this loop hike, followed by a longer, gradual descent and a final short section that is nearly level.

Printing the Map

Always carry a printed copy of your digital map on the trip. Make sure your mapping program is set to print map grids in the coordinate system that your GPS is displaying. Grids make it easier to mark waypoints on the printed map in the field. For longer excursions such as backpacking, river running, or sea kayaking, you may have to print multiple pages to cover the entire route. Overlap the edges slightly, and number the sheets in trip sequence.

Maps printed from an ink jet printer are not waterproof unless they're printed with waterproof ink on special paper. Maps printed on laser printers are more water resistant, but it's still good to store the folded maps in plastic bags.

Uploading to the GPS

Once you have the trip plotted to your satisfaction, it's time to upload it to your GPS receiver. First, connect the receiver to your computer with a USB cable and turn it on. Next, use the GPS setup feature to tell your mapping program which GPS brand and model you have, as well as the connection type. Finally, use the upload or export to GPS function to send the data to the GPS.

Something to think about is whether you want to clear all the previous GPS data from the unit before uploading a new trip. Since it can be slow and confusing to search through a lot of waypoints and routes, and track memory is limited, for e-hiking it's better to clear the GPS receiver's memory before uploading a new trip. It's a good idea to download all the data from your GPS to your computer immediately after a trip, so you can safely erase the GPS for the next trip.

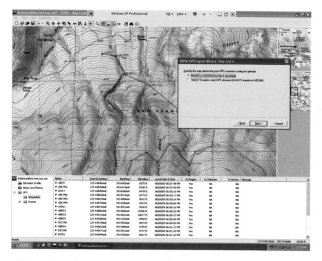

When uploading your routes and waypoints to the GPS, it is critical that you pick the correct datum to avoid serious position errors. Digital maps normally use WGS84.

Chapter Five

Road Navigation

Road navigation using a street GPS consists of finding a point of interest (POI) and telling the unit you want to go there. A POI is a waypoint that is either already in the database, or added later by the user. Current street GPSs have millions of POIs, including restaurants, gas stations, airports, lodging, shopping, banks and ATMs, parking, entertainment, recreation, attractions, medical services, government offices, auto services, and many others. If a POI is not in the database, you can find a location by street address or intersection, browse the map to find a location, or enter coordinates directly.

FINDING POINTS OF INTEREST

Searching by Type

The easiest way to find a POI when you don't know the name but do know the type of place you're looking for, such as a motel or a restaurant, is to search by type. The GPS assumes you want to search near your present location—if this is not the case, you can search along your route, at your destination, or in a different city. Just select the Points of Interest icon, then the type of POI and category. The GPS presents a list sorted by distance from your selected location, and also indicates the direction. Once you choose a POI, you'll have options to view the POI on a map, or save it to your favorites.

This screen shows some of the POI types you can search. For more choices, touch the down arrow. You can search by name, and you can specify where you want to search—near your destination along the route, where you are now, or near another place. Of course, POIs change, so you'll want to frequently download and install a new POI database from the GPS manufacturer, especially before a major road trip.

Searching by Name

You can also search by name, which is easy when you know the specific name of a POI, such as Joe's Fast Food. Again, the GPS assumes you want to search near your present location—if this is not the case, you can search elsewhere. Enter as much of the name as you know. The unit presents a list sorted by distance from your selected location, and also shows the direction. You have the same options to view the POI on a map, or save it to your favorites.

Flagstaff Pulliam Airport

6200 S Pulliam Dr
Flagstaff, AZ 86001
928-556-1234

Route Info
Distance: 6.9 mi
Time: 12 mins
Fuel Cost: $0.49

Go!

Back   Map   Save

Saving a POI in the GPS unit's memory saves a lot of time the next time you want to go to the same place. A saved POI can be a POI in the unit's database, or a custom POI you've entered and named yourself.

Searching Favorites and Recently Found

These two lists are far shorter than the main POI database and are searched much faster. You also have the options to view the POI on a map, or edit it to change the name or symbol.

USING A STREET GPS TO FIND A TRAILHEAD

Since trailheads are rarely found in POI databases, you will probably have to enter coordinates. You can get the coordinates from a printed map, but the

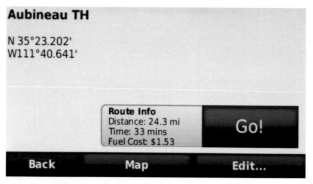

Aubineau TH

N 35°23.202'
W111°40.641'

Route Info
Distance: 24.3 mi
Time: 33 mins
Fuel Cost: $1.53

Go!

Back   Map   Edit...

This trailhead was manually entered using coordinates taken from a USGS topo map, and can now be selected like any other POI. This street GPS shows the route's distance, time, and fuel cost.

easiest way is to locate the trailhead on a digital map. Just point to the trailhead location with the mouse and read the coordinates from the display. Be very careful as you manually enter the coordinates into the street GPS—cross-check that you've entered the correct numbers several times. A typo could take you to a place miles from the trailhead. Then save the location as a favorite, using a name that describes the trailhead. Now you can pick the trailhead from your favorites list and navigate directly to it.

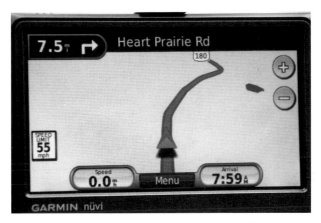

On the way to the trailhead using a street GPS, the display shows
a turn from the highway onto a dirt national forest road coming
up on the right in 7.5 miles. The road name, Hart, is misspelled in
the GPS database.

Chapter Six

Trail Navigation

When hiking a trail, you can use your GPS in either of two ways. You can leave it off most of the time, only turning it on when you'd like to check your progress or mark a trail junction or other landmark. This is a good choice when you don't need to save an actual track log of the route, or you need to save your batteries on a multiday trip. Battery life is so good on most trail GPS receivers that you can save hundreds of waypoints using this method and still have the batteries last for a week or more. Be sure your unit is set to battery save mode, if it has one.

CHECKING THE GPS'S ACCURACY

At the start of any trip, it's important to turn the unit on and give it plenty of time to get a solid position fix, especially if the receiver has been moved more than 100 miles since it was last used. GPS receivers keep an almanac, a record of the position of the GPS satellites, in their memories, and this data has to be updated from the satellite signals if the GPS hasn't been used recently. Although current GPS receivers are designed to lock on to the satellites in less than a minute in a "cold start," less than ideal conditions, such as tree cover, may cause it to take longer. Later

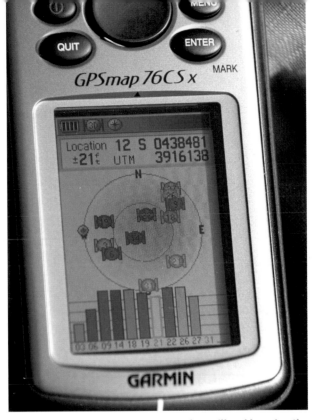

Check the GPS receiver's accuracy at the trailhead by using the satellite status page before starting your trip. Icons along the top of the screen show that it is running on battery power, it has a 3D fix, and the electronic compass is on. Other icons appear when the unit is plugged into a computer, the backlight is on, or WAAS is active. The next line shows the estimated position accuracy, 21 feet, and your current position. The graphic below shows the position of the satellites in the sky and their signal strengths. Solid colors indicate satellites that are locked and being used for navigation, while gray icons and bars show satellites that are not locked. Here, satellites 21 and 31 are not locked. As you move, the status page changes to show the quality of the satellite lock. GPS needs at least four locked satellites for a 3D navigation fix.

startups on the same day (a "warm start") take only a few seconds unless the sky is partly obscured.

Use the satellite status page to check the unit's accuracy. The receiver needs to be locked on to at least three satellites in order to navigate (some units call this a 2D fix), but four or more is the minimum for the unit to compute both altitude and position (called a 3D fix). You should ensure the unit has a 3D fix before marking critical waypoints, such as the trailhead. Some units also show an estimated horizontal accuracy—this should be 33 feet (10 meters) or less. If the unit is having difficulty getting an accurate fix, move to a place with a better view of the sky.

MARKING THE TRAILHEAD

It is very important that you mark the trailhead or your starting point before moving away. Don't depend on a waypoint you've downloaded or marked on a map. Save the trailhead location using the mark waypoint function on the GPS. The unit will assign a default waypoint name such as 001 or WPT001. As you save waypoints, the receiver increments the number. Just remember that waypoint 001 is the trailhead or starting point.

Marking the trailhead by pressing and holding the Enter/Mark button on this unit results in a waypoint with the default name 001. The note field contains the date and time, and your location and elevation are shown. Pressing Enter saves the waypoint, or you can use the four-way pad to select Avg (position averaging) if you want to increase the accuracy of the waypoint.

POSITION AVERAGING

Some units let you improve waypoint accuracy by averaging a number of position fixes over time. You must be stationary for this to work. Averaging can be especially helpful when you don't have a good view of the sky and the accuracy is less than the standard 33 feet (10 meters).

FIELD NAMING OF WAYPOINTS

You can change the default name of a waypoint using the GPS buttons or touch screen icons, but it's time consuming. A better way is to accept the default names and make notes describing the waypoint, using a notepad or the back of a printed map. Or you can use a digital voice recorder to make notes on the go, which is easier when paddling a boat or riding a bike.

RECORDING A TRACK LOG

A track log is a series of waypoints that are automatically saved by the GPS while the unit is on. You can't see the waypoints in a track log, but most units let you name and save the track log. Record a track log whenever you want a continuous record of your route—hiking a trail that's not mapped or snowshoeing cross-country, for example. Also, if you

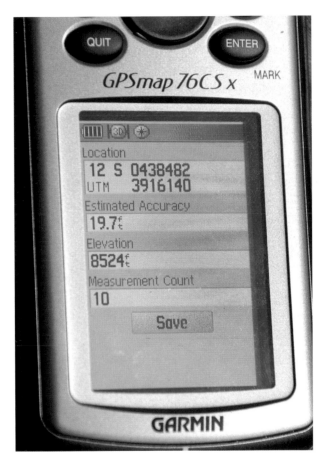

This position-averaging screen shows an estimated accuracy of 19.7 feet after ten measurements have been made. The longer you wait, the more accurate the fix. You can also improve the accuracy by moving slightly to get a better view of the sky, but then you'll have to stay in one place so the unit can average the position fixes.

have a track log, you can use the GPS to follow the track back to your starting point.

You should begin with a new track log at the start of a trip. Do this from the track log setup page by saving your existing track log, if you haven't already, and then clearing the track log. Make sure the track log function is turned on.

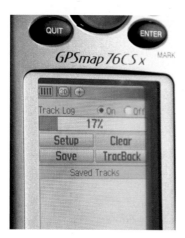

This track log screen shows that the track log function is turned on and that 17 percent of the track log is being used. Before starting a new trip, you'll want to save the old track log and start a new one by clearing the track log. This page also shows the Trac-Back feature, which lets you retrace your route using the track log.

TRIP COMPUTER PAGE

You should reset this page at the start of the trip so the data accurately reflects the current trip. Also, reset the elevation data at the same time. Again, the GPS has to be left on continuously for this data to mean anything.

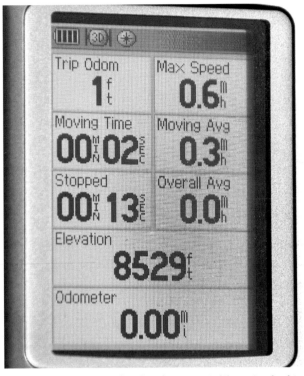

This trip computer page has just been reset. It's customized to show maximum, moving average, and current speeds; moving and stopped times; elevation; and odometer. It shows maximum speed, moving average speed, and overall average speed. This page also shows moving and stopped times, the odometer for this trip, and an overall odometer at the bottom. It may be useful to customize one of the data fields, such as the bottom odometer, to show speed instead.

CARRYING THE GPS

Except when moving though heavy brush or exceptionally rough terrain, you'll want the GPS receiver accessible while you travel. If you plan to record a track log, the GPS needs to be kept on and mounted where it will have a view of the sky. Otherwise, you can just keep it in a place that's accessible without having to stop. Some packs have pockets that can be reached while you're hiking.

This GPS is mounted on the pack's right shoulder strap so it has a good view of the sky and can be reached without removing the pack. This is a handy way to carry a GPS even of you don't leave it on continuously. The case is a neoprene pouch designed for handheld radio transceivers. A hook-and-loop strap secures the GPS in place, and a hook-and-loop band attaches it to the shoulder strap.

Kayakers and other paddlers can use a deck bag, and cyclists can use a handlebar mount.

NAVIGATING ROUTES

Navigation on a preloaded route is started by calling up the route page, selecting the desired route, and activating it. If you plan to follow the route in the opposite direction than you entered it into the GPS, you can reverse the route using the route menu. This is also useful if you're partway along a planned hike and have to turn back.

When you activate the route, the GPS will start navigating to the first waypoint in the route. Switch to the map page to see a graphic representation of your route. You can zoom in to focus on the area near your present position, or zoom out for a wider look. You can also pan the map away from your present location by using the four-way controller (the large central button found on most GPS receivers with keypads). Exit pan mode by pressing Quit.

CHANGING A WAYPOINT IN A ROUTE

If your preplanned trailhead waypoint is wrong, as shown by the location of the trailhead waypoint you just saved at the actual trailhead, you should change the old trailhead waypoint in your route to the new one, which in this case is 001. If you're doing a loop

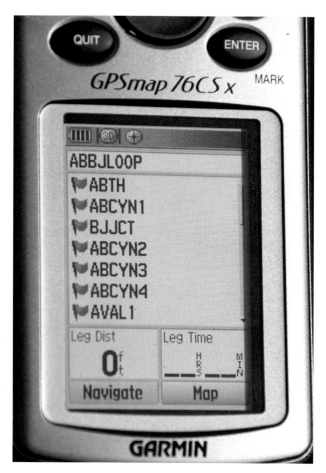

The top line of this route page shows the name of the selected route, and the main window shows a list of the waypoints in the route. By moving the highlight down the list of waypoints, you can see the leg distance and time (if moving). Navigation proceeds to each waypoint in turn until the end of the route is reached.

trip, change the end waypoint to waypoint 001. Using the route edit screen, you can review the saved information for a waypoint, insert a new waypoint, and remove, change, or move an existing waypoint.

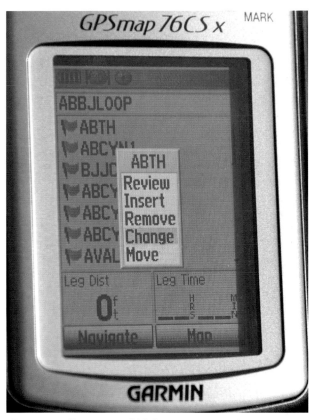

The route edit screen, which lets you review, insert, remove, change, or move a waypoint in the route.

NAVIGATING TO WAYPOINTS

When hiking along a trail, or any other time you aren't free to travel directly toward a waypoint, the map page is probably the screen you'll use most. If you've set up the map page to orient "track up," then your current direction of travel is always toward the top of the screen. (Some GPS units can be set to change to "north up" below a certain speed. It's useful to have north up when you're stopped.) Your current location is shown in the center of the screen, and the waypoints along the route are shown, connected by a line. You can see at a glance your progress in relation to the next waypoint.

The compass screen is also useful, depending on how you have it set up. Distance and time to the next waypoint and to your destination are good data to have, as this gives you an idea when to expect to reach the next waypoint, as well as your destination. Keep in mind that the distances and times may be less than the actual distance and time required to reach a waypoint if the trail takes an indirect route. Generally, marking a preplanned route with as many waypoints as possible increases the accuracy of the displayed distance and time.

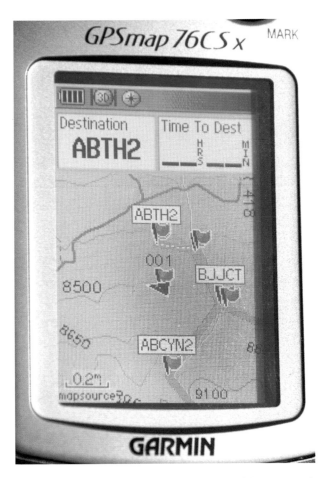

This map page displays a graphic presentation of the route, with waypoints shown. This is the most useful page when hiking a trail or defined route. Since we're not moving, the map is displayed north up. Notice that the preplanned location of the trailhead (ABTH2) is wrong. Waypoint 001 was saved at the car and is the actual location of the trailhead.

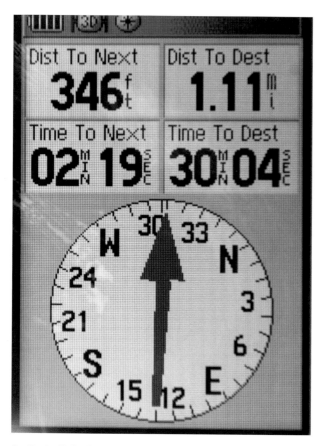

On the trail the GPS compass page helps keep you oriented, and also shows your progress. This screen is set up to show the distance and time to the next waypoint and to the final destination. The compass rose shows your heading (the actual direction you're traveling), and the red arrow shows the bearing to the next waypoint. This may not be the same as your current heading if the trail is switchbacking or otherwise not taking a direct line to the next waypoint.

SAVING WAYPOINTS AS YOU TRAVEL

Remember to mark waypoints as you travel by stopping at key points such as trail junctions and points of interest and using the mark position function. Even if you're recording a track log to map a trail and upload it to your computer, it's important to manually save waypoints. Manually saved waypoints are more accurate than track log waypoints, especially if your GPS has a position averaging feature. Also, manual waypoints are named and can be edited. If you're not recording a track log, or have the GPS turned off most of the time, it's even more important to record waypoints as you go. Remember to make notes about each waypoint, so that after the trip you'll know the purpose of each one.

Chapter Seven
Point to Point Navigation

Point to point navigation is traveling directly to each waypoint in turn. Examples are cross-country hiking, sea kayaking, backcountry skiing, or any other activity where you're not following a defined road or trail.

TRAVELING ALONG A BEARING

Unless your GPS receiver has a calibrated magnetic compass, it's difficult to use a GPS to travel along a bearing in a straight line, especially at walking speeds. The GPS bearing is erratic at low speeds, so you should use a handheld compass.

Start by traveling a bearing directly to the next waypoint, using the GPS magnetic compass or handheld compass to determine the bearing to that waypoint. Then pick out a landmark along your direction of travel that is as far away as possible and travel directly toward it. Check your progress by occasionally referring to the GPS or handheld compass. Don't try to travel by constantly referring to either device. It's hard to travel a straight line this way, and your eyes should be on the ground watching for hazards and working out your line of travel. Even when paddling a boat, it's much easier to travel in a straight line by using a distant reference. Of course, if visibility is limited by terrain or weather, you may have no choice except to use the GPS or handheld compass.

The compass screen is presented differently on various GPS models. Some units have a circular compass ring just like a handheld compass. In this case the outer ring rotates to show your direction of travel under the lubber line at the top center of the compass, and a bearing arrow rotates independently to show the bearing to the next waypoint.

To travel directly to a waypoint using the compass page on the GPS, turn until the red bearing arrow is pointed in the same direction you're moving, which is normally straight ahead.

Other GPS models may have a highway-type compass screen, where you turn until the highway is straight ahead of you on the screen, or an edge view compass, which shows a strip of compass directions moving across the screen.

To use a handheld compass to follow a bearing, first read the bearing to the next waypoint from the GPS screen. Then set the rotating outer ring of the handheld compass to the desired bearing (this assumes you have a compass with a declination adjustment that is set correctly for your area so that the compass reads true bearings, rather than magnetic bearings). Hold the compass level in front of you, with the lubber line at the top of the compass pointing away, then turn until the north end of the needle lines up with the magnetic north reference on the compass baseplate. Sight over the compass and pick out a landmark that is as far away as possible, and travel toward it.

DEALING WITH OBSTACLES

Sometimes, in open country or on the water, you can actually travel in a straight line. Often, though, you'll have to deviate from your course (the bearing line you want to travel) for obstacles such as islands, reefs, or canyons. Or the country may be so rough that you can never travel in a straight line for more than a few minutes.

This is where it helps to have picked out a distant landmark along your bearing line. If you can keep the

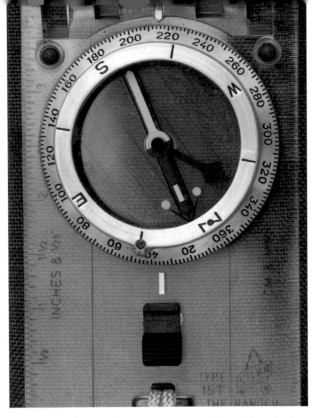

On this baseplate-style mapping compass, the rotating ring has been set to a bearing of 215 degrees, or approximately southwest. Turn your body and the compass until the north end of the compass needle is lined up with the black arrow on the baseplate. Note that the black arrow is offset about 13 degrees from north as marked on the rotating ring. This adjustment is made by turning the small brass screw located next to the 45-degree point until the black arrow shows the magnetic declination for the area, in degrees east or west of true north. You can find the declination for your area on the data block in the lower left corner of USGS topo maps. You can also get it by temporarily setting your GPS to read magnetic bearings, and reading it from the setup screen. Don't forget to set the GPS back to true.

landmark in sight, you can deviate all you want, as long as you head generally toward your landmark.

If you can't see very far, pick two landmarks, such as two trees or a tree and a rock outcrop, that line up ahead along your course. Keep the two landmarks lined up as you travel. If you have to deviate to one side to avoid a small obstacle, then turn the opposite way until the two landmarks line up again. When you reach the first landmark, pick a third one beyond the second, so you'll always have two landmarks visible ahead.

This technique can be used when there are no landmarks visible at all—a foggy water or glacier crossing, for example—if several other members of your party can act as landmarks. On the water with a group of canoes or kayaks, place a couple of boats ahead of you, but close enough that you can communicate with the lead boater. Then call out "left" or "right" to direct the lead boater to turn slightly as you monitor your heading with a GPS compass, marine compass, or handheld compass. This technique works similarly on a foggy snowfield or glacier by placing a couple of people out ahead within sight and hearing.

Refer to the map page occasionally as you travel. Since it shows your desired course as well as your actual track and present position, you can see how far off course you might be.

MARKING WAYPOINTS ON A PAPER MAP

You should know how to manually plot your position on a printed map. Although the advent of GPS units with large-scale topo maps is making this skill less necessary, it is still useful if you are outside the mapping coverage of your GPS, or if your printed topo map is more accurate than the map on your GPS.

It's easier to plot your position on printed digital maps if you set your computer mapping program to print at 1:24,000 or larger scale and to print a 1,000-meter UTM grid. Also set your GPS to display UTM coordinates. Then you can use the grid and the kilometer distance scale at the bottom of the map to estimate your position within about 50 meters (165 feet). For more accuracy you can use a UTM plotter (see my other GPS book, *Basic Essentials Using GPS*), but for recreational use the plotterless method is usually accurate enough.

Some paper topo or recreation maps are printed with UTM or lat/long grids. *Remember to set the GPS's datum to the map datum.* If the datum is not marked on the map, use WGS84, which is the new worldwide standard for mapping.

If the map is not gridded, you can still estimate your position within about 200 meters (650 feet), depending on the map scale, by using the UTM ticks along the map margin and the kilometer scale at the bottom of the map. It helps to use the edge of a piece of paper, or another map, to transfer measurements from the kilometer scale to the map.

If your map only has lat/long coordinates, estimating waypoints is a little tougher, because the lat/long lines do not form a rectangular grid. It's possible to estimate lat/long coordinates by eye, but you'll be hard pressed to be more accurate than about 400 meters (0.25 mile). It helps to pregrid the paper map with lat/long lines, but for real accuracy you'll need a special lat/long plotter for your map's scale. A few such sessions are enough to convince most people that UTM is far better for field use.

If your paper map has no coordinate system at all, don't try to use it for GPS navigation—or any outdoor navigation. Get a better map.

You can also read GPS coordinates from a printed map in the field and manually enter them into your GPS. This may be necessary when you need to travel to a location that you didn't save as a waypoint during your pretrip planning. Use the same general technique described earlier, only in reverse. Doing this tedious procedure a few times should quickly convince you of the value of planning your trip at home and uploading the digital map waypoints directly to your GPS.

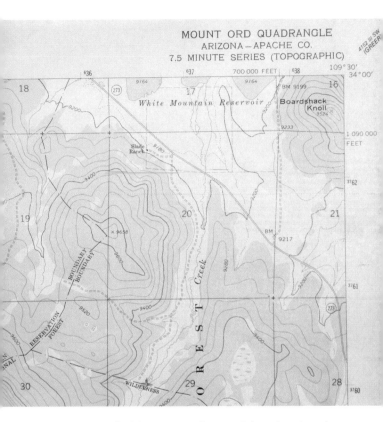

Here we want to find the UTM coordinates of the point where the creek meets the wilderness boundary at the center lower edge of the map, as marked by a small cross. Using the UTM tick marks along the top and right margins, we estimate the coordinates to be 636600E 3760100N. Read Zone 12 from the text on the lower left corner of the map (see photo of USGS map detail in Chapter 3). This map uses the NAD27 datum, so make sure you set your mapping program and GPS unit to NAD27 before entering these coordinates.

NAVIGATING DIRECTLY TO A WAYPOINT

So far we've been navigating to waypoints contained in a route. You can also navigate directly to any waypoint in your GPS, including one you've estimated in the field from a paper map and entered manually into the GPS. An extreme example would be if you got completely lost and decided to go directly back to the trailhead.

More likely, you spot something of interest on your paper or GPS map and decide to go directly to it. First, enter the new waypoint manually if it's not already in the GPS. Next, press the Go To or Find button or icon on your GPS, then select the desired waypoint. Select "Go To" from the waypoint screen, and then you can navigate to the waypoint just like any other waypoint. Or from the map page, scroll to the desired waypoint and press Enter.

As you arrive at a waypoint, the GPS will beep and flash a message on the screen. You can verify your arrival at the waypoint on the map page of the GPS.

WEAK OR LOST GPS SIGNAL

When the sky is partially obscured, such as in heavy forest or a deep canyon, the GPS may not see enough satellites to navigate. If your unit loses its lock while you are moving, try stopping in the most open spot

Heavy forest cover may block GPS reception and cause the satellite lock to be lost, especially while moving. A GPS receiver works by picking up extremely faint, line-of-sight radio signals from satellites that are 12,000 or more miles distant.

you can find. GPS receivers have a much easier time maintaining a satellite lock if they are stationary. In some cases, such as in the extremely narrow slot canyons of the American Southwest, a GPS receiver is completely useless. On the other hand, GPS technology keeps improving, and current GPS receivers are much more sensitive than older units. Modern receivers can track twelve or more satellites simultaneously, which greatly improves their ability to navigate under difficult conditions.

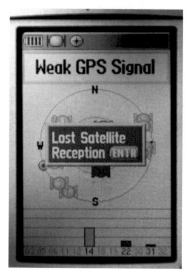

A warning pops up on the screen when satellite reception is weak or lost, and most units will beep as well. Move to a place with a better view of the sky.

Chapter Eight

Recording and Sharing Your Trip

After your trip you'll want to download the GPS data to your digital maps; add comments, photos, or videos; and share it with others. You can also download your trip data to Google Earth, which lets you see your trip on satellite imagery and also share it.

DOWNLOADING GPS DATA TO YOUR DIGITAL MAP

This example uses National Geographic Topo!, but you can do this with other digital maps as well. See Chapter 1 for a summary of digital map products—off-line, online, and smartphone.

Turn your GPS on and plug it into a USB port on the computer. Open Topo!, then open the import dialog and select the data you wish to download. Normally this would be waypoints and tracks, but you can also import routes if you created new ones on the trip. You'll be asked how you want to import the track log. The choices let you import the log as waypoints, as a new route line each time the GPS had to search the sky for satellites, or as a continuous route line.

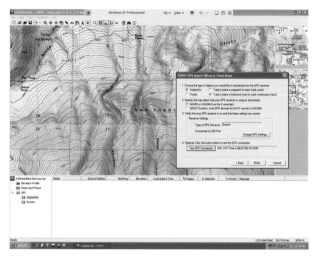

To download your GPS data to your computer using Topo!, start with a new map—that is, a map without any GPS or route data. Then open the import dialog and select the data you want to download, which is usually waypoints and tracks. You can also download routes if you created new ones in the field.

TOPO! © 2010 NATIONAL GEOGRAPHIC

If you cleared the track log in the GPS at the start of the trip, then import the track log as a continuous route line. If you have done several trips since you cleared the track log, then import the track log as a new route line each time the GPS searched the sky. This shows each trip as a separate route line on the map. A continuous route would connect the separate trips with a route line, which could be miles long if your trips were widely separated. Again you can see why it's best to clear the GPS track log at the start of each trip.

The remaining option lets you import the GPS track log as a series of automatically named waypoints. This is useful if you wish to manipulate the track log on the map by renaming the waypoints or creating a route. Be aware that you'll get a lot of waypoints.

When the download is complete, the imported waypoints will be shown on the map and in the waypoint list. You can double-click on a waypoint in the list to jump to that waypoint on the map. (You'll probably have to zoom in to see your trip, unless you covered a lot of ground.) The track log shows up as a route line on the map.

Managing Waypoints

If you've been using the system in this book so far, the waypoints that you created during your pretrip planning on the computer will have unique names, and the waypoints you created on the trip will have automatic names (001, 002, 003, etc.). You'll want to delete any pretrip waypoints that are incorrect. In this example the original pre-trip ABTH and ABTH2 waypoints at the trailhead turned out to be incorrect, as a new trailhead had been built. At the start of the trip, you saved the actual trailhead location as waypoint 001. Delete ABTH from the map and rename 001 to ABTH. Using your field waypoint notes, rename all the other field waypoints to meaningful names. This is done in Topo! by right-clicking on the waypoint on the map or in the waypoint list, and choosing Properties from the pop-up menu. (See the Topo! Waypoint Editor screen image in Chapter 4 for an example.) Although the waypoint name is limited by your GPS receiver's memory, keep in mind that you can put a description in the message field of the Properties box. The GPS used in this example allows thirteen characters for the waypoint name and thirty in the message field. Most GPS units put the date and time the waypoint was saved into the message field, and you add to this data or overwrite it.

Adding Notes and Photos to the Map

In Topo! you can use the Notes and Photos tool to make notes, add photos, and link Web locations (URLs) to the map. (National Geographic Topo! Explorer also lets you link videos.) This tool places a small icon on the map and opens an area at the bottom of the screen where you can type in text. Click on the Photo button to link to a photo on your hard drive, and the Link button to add a Web link. The Location and Visibility button controls which map levels show the icon, and the Shortcut only check box hides the icon. You can place as many Notes and Photos icons on the map as you wish. The note also serves as a shortcut to the map. Clicking on the note in the list centers the map on the icon, and changes the map to the scale in which it was created.

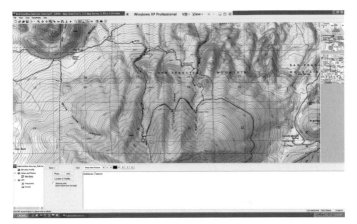

The track log from the GPS is shown in red on the map; way-points are in blue. Rename the field waypoints (001, 002, etc.) to meaningful names. Then use the Notes and Photos tool to add text notes and link photos to the map. A note has been added at the bottom of the map just north of the Lunch waypoint with the text "Aubineau Canyon."

TOPO! © 2010 NATIONAL GEOGRAPHIC

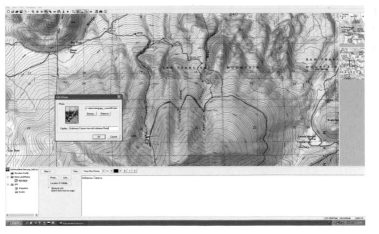

A photo of Aubineau Canyon has been linked to this note.

TOPO! © 2010 NATIONAL GEOGRAPHIC

UPLOADING TO GOOGLE EARTH

You can upload GPS data directly from your GPS receiver to Google Earth by connecting the GPS to your computer, then selecting GPS from the Tools menu. Select the device and the items you want to import—waypoints, tracks, or routes, and then the options. Check "Adjust altitudes to ground level." Then click the Import button.

You can upload your waypoints to Google Earth from National Geographic Topo! or another program by saving the waypoint file as a GPX file and then

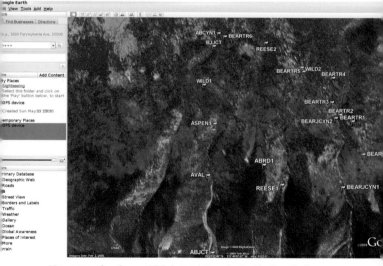

You can upload your GPS data to Google Earth directly from supported GPS receivers or from any computer mapping program that can export GPS data as a GPX file.

dragging and dropping the file into Google Earth. The GPS waypoints show in the image window, and a list appears in the sidebar under My Places, GPS device. You should rename the GPS device to reflect the name of your trip.

SHARING YOUR TRIP

It's easy to share your GPS trip data with other people, either off-line or online. This example uses National Geographic Topo! and Topo! Explorer, but there are many other programs you can use, including Google Earth and DeLorme Topo North America.

National Geographic Topo!

You can share your Topo! trip with other users of Topo! by sending them the TPO file by e-mail or on a CD. They can view your file even if they don't have maps of the area, but of course it's more useful if they do. Linked photos won't show up, so it's better to post your photos on a Web photo-sharing site and then link to them using the Links button in the Notes and Photos tool.

National Geographic Topo! Explorer

Before you can share a trip online using Topo! Explorer, you have to either create a trip in Topo! Explorer using its tools, or upload trip data from National Geographic Topo! by importing a TPO file.

Then you can edit the trip, add photos and videos, and share it on www.topo.com.

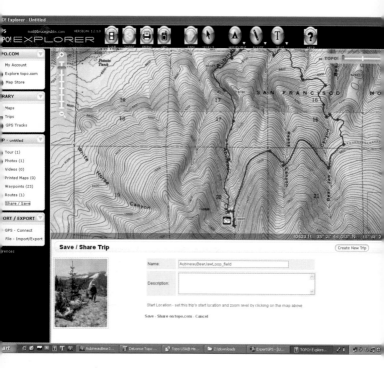

You can share a trip you created in National Geographic Topo! by opening it in Topo! Explorer, or by creating a new trip in Topo! Explorer. Use the tools in Topo! Explorer to add photos and videos. To share your trip, use the Share/Save tool on the left sidebar to upload your trip to the Web site at www.topo.com.

TOPO! EXPLORER © 2010 NATIONAL GEOGRAPHIC

Chapter Nine
Geocaching

Geocaching is an outdoor treasure hunting sport that uses a GPS receiver to find geocaches. A geocache is a small container hidden by someone that holds a notepad for logging your comments. Some geocaches are themed; others include small trinkets that you can exchange for one of your own. The worldwide geocaching Web site is www.geocaching .com. There are over a million geocaches worldwide in both urban and rural areas. Once you've located a geocache, you can go back on the Web site and log your find as well as read comments from others.

Benchmarking is a related activity also supported on www.geocaching.com. Benchmarks are permanent survey markers established on the ground by government agencies for mapping and surveying.

GEOCACHING

After you register for a free membership on www .geocaching.com, you can search for geocaches by street address, zip code, state, country, lat/ long, name, and several other methods. Read the description and clues for finding the geocache and download the geocache waypoint files (in LOC format) to your computer. You can then upload the geocache waypoints directly to your GPS, or import them to a mapping program.

DeLorme Topo North America and ExpertGPS are the best digital map programs for geocaching because they can import geocache LOC files directly. You can import LOC files into National Geographic Topo! and Topo! Explorer by converting to GPX format, but you lose all of the geocache data except the waypoint location. Although you don't have to import geocache waypoints to your mapping program, it adds to the fun to do so.

The geocaching Web site can upload geocache data directly to geocache-supported GPS receivers. All mapping GPS units support geocaching with special icons and features, and come with support programs that can read geocache LOC files for direct upload to the computer. You can also mark a geocache as found and enter notes directly into the GPS unit. With non-mapping, GPS receivers, you may need to use a program such as EasyGPS (which is free) to read the LOC files and upload them to your receiver.

A typical geocache in a waterproof, screw-top plastic jar. This geocache contains a log and several small trinkets.

You'll need the description and clues from www .geocaching.com because your GPS only gets you within about 33 feet of the geocache. In complex terrain or urban areas, that can still leave a lot of hiding places. Once you find the geocache, follow the instructions inside and then replace it exactly as you found it. You may want to read the comments left by others in the logbook, as well as make your own comments.

Back at your computer, you can log your experience with the geocache you found. Your log entry can specify that the geocache was found, not found, needs maintenance, or archive.

BENCHMARKING

Benchmarks are mapped points established on the ground by government surveyors anytime a precise location is needed. Commonly a benchmark is a small metal disk set in a rock outcrop or a cement block, but other structures such as radio towers and church spires are also used. Many benchmarks are part of the national control network used as a reference for mapping the country, while others are placed to support major projects such as highways and dams.

Although many agencies place benchmarks, the National Geodetic Survey (NGS) maintains a database of all known benchmarks. This database is accessible to the public via the benchmarking link on www.geocaching.com, and currently has more than

730,000 benchmarks. You can search for benchmarks and download waypoint files to your computer and GPS in the same manner as geocaches. While the NGS database is read-only, www.geocaching.com maintains a public log where you can describe your experience finding a benchmark.

While most benchmarks are located in urban areas and next to roads, many are in remote areas that can only be reached by trail or cross-country hiking. Quite a few have never been visited by government surveyors since they were originally placed, and many are more than a century old. For more information, visit the benchmarking link at www.geocaching.com.

This benchmark was placed in 1903 on the South Rim of the Grand Canyon by the U.S. Geological Survey during the original topographic mapping of the canyon. Surveying was accomplished by arduous foot and mule travel into some of the most rugged terrain on Earth. This historic benchmark hasn't been visited by government surveyors since then.

Chapter Ten
The Future

Paper maps are a unique combination of technical and artistic expertise that have been part of human civilization since the beginning. The communication, navigation, and computer revolution is bringing change to mapping and navigation at an unbelievable rate, and it's clear that the map of the future will be an interactive electronic document, viewed on a high-resolution, power-sipping device. Current smartphone apps are just the tip of the iceberg. Imagine an electronic map device with the lightweight and extended battery life of an e-book reader and the size and vivid color screen of a tablet computer, along with world-wide satellite Internet connectivity. These maps will know where you are, thanks to GPS, and also have integrated images, video, and sound. You'll be able to switch seamlessly between topo map views and satellite and aerial photography, and wirelessly upload and download trip data. But paper maps will always have their place as a backup, just as electronic compasses will never completely replace mechanical compasses. After all, the batteries never die on a paper map.

It's easy, in our hyper-gadget-bound culture, to get so enamored of our neat little devices that we lose sight of the big picture—the reason we are out in the backcountry is to enjoy being in the backcountry. A backpacker with a do-it-all navigator/electronic map/e-mail/texting/camera/video/musicplayer/ Web surfer smartphone is kind of like camping in the woods in a motorhome. What's the point of getting away from it all if you bring it all with you?

Index